You

# You Name It

## Colin Herd

Dostoyevsky Wannabe Originals
*An Imprint of Dostoyevsky Wannabe*

First Published in 2019
by Dostoyevsky Wannabe Originals
All rights reserved
© Colin Herd

Dostoyevsky Wannabe Originals is an imprint of
Dostoyevsky Wannabe publishing.

www.dostoyevskywannabe.com

This book is a work of fiction. The names, characters and incidents portrayed in it are the work of the authors' imagination. Any resemblance to actual persons, living or dead, events or localities is entirely coincidental.

Cover design by Dostoyevsky Wannabe Design

ISBN-9781704980874


No parts of this publication may be reproduced, stored in a retrieval system, or transmitted in any form or by any means, electronic, mechanical, photocopying, recording, or otherwise, without the prior written permission of the copyright owner.

This book is sold subject to the condition that it shall not, by way of trade or otherwise, be lent, resold, hired out, or otherwise circulated without the publisher's prior consent in any form of binding or cover other than that in which it is published and without a similar condition including this condition being imposed on the subsequent purchaser. Under no circumstances may any part of this book be photocopied for resale.

## Contents

| | |
|---|---|
| Fanciphobia | 11 |
| Midsummer Wet Dream / Soggy Nightmare | 16 |
| When I eat yoghurt | 17 |
| Colonoscopy | 19 |
| Reifying Desire 3, Jacolby Satterwhite (2013) | 21 |
| It's very early | 24 |
| Epistemo-erotic Advantage | 25 |
| Definitely wear trainers! | 27 |
| Your Barking Lesson | 29 |
| Mozartian | 30 |
| Imprint | 31 |
| Kissed by Bubbles | 33 |
| Hi Mum I'm in a Poem, Just… | 39 |
| Softness | 40 |
| Zebra and Parachute, Christopher Wood | 41 |
| So many poems | 42 |
| Landing | 43 |
| I can't do it alone, want to join in? | 44 |
| The word unputdownable | 45 |
| My new friend has a bathtub | 47 |
| Thorn Bug Huff-Song | 49 |
| Bubbles Galore (1996), dir. Cynthia Roberts | 50 |
| Fudge Packer | 56 |
| after Bully and Bitch, Asim Butt (2008) | 58 |
| Hesitation Cocktail | 59 |

| | |
|---|---|
| Hint hint | 60 |
| Email me tomorrow morning or else | 61 |
| My car is an unreliable narrator | 62 |
| My Humiliation Fetish | 64 |
| A wrapper | 65 |
| Weird Fight | 67 |
| Sir Walter Scott | 68 |
| A Famous Singer's Mother | 70 |
| Punching Time | 71 |
| As Much As I love It | 72 |
| Rome was not like you see in the movies | 73 |
| Raw and Boiled Tongue | 74 |
| Our Light and Our Fan | 76 |
| Two sweaters for one person or one sweater for more than one | 77 |
| TV Hairline Perk | 78 |
| Meadowbank Changing Manifesto | 80 |
| Nice Honk, Van Driver | 82 |
| after an image of Kaarlo Sarkia | 83 |
| My Mystical Love Poetry | 84 |
| after Truong Tan, 'When Love Starts', 2006 | 86 |
| Laplaplaplaplaplaplap Top | 87 |
| ? + Fiat | 93 |
| Rough | 94 |
| Coup de Pied | 98 |
| Behind a Mustang | 99 |
| Two non-starters | 100 |

| | |
|---|---|
| Plateau's Laws | 102 |
| And now you're all thinking | |
| Who said anything about enjoyment? | 104 |
| The Pond Aflame | 107 |
| Male Nude, 1934, Duncan Grant | 109 |
| Streusel Topping | 111 |
| Area Scatter | 112 |
| Dream Fettucine | 117 |
| Woolf Bubbles for Colin Herd on his Birthday | 135 |
| Syllabubble | 141 |

## Acknowledgements

Some of these poems have previously been published in Granta, MAKAR/UNMAKAR, Spam, Gilded Dirt, Hwearf, Gutter, Virginia Woolf and the World of Books and Magma. 'Fanciphobia' is inspired by Jeffrey Robinson's book Unfettering Poetry: The Fancy in British Romanticism. The other many influences and acknowledgments are badged pretty clearly in the text. This book is intended as a kind of swoon - a falling in love with queer art everyday. I sort of love it when Diane Wakoski says in Toward a New Poetry: "Any conversation with anybody about poetry is very exciting to me - and sexual. Because poetry is a metaphor for sex for me, or sex is a metaphor for poetry or whatever. At a certain point the imagination has transformed the event so it doesn't make any difference. I suppose being a materialist I think it all comes out of the libido and therefore is initially physical." I hope you enjoy this book and if you do, tell everybody.

**Fanciphobia**

hello all of you
brilliant poets and poetry fans
such appetites etc
I was thinking
tomorrow morning
how about you
walk out of your jobs
and those without jobs walk into them
just up and toodle-ooo
just up and hello nice to meet you
take the staple gun
fantasize interiors
my name all of a sudden is
if you could redecorate
one thing
my name all of a sudden is
I want to quit my job
and start negotiating
(I like my job)
take the coffee machine
that's going nowhere
trellised rose wall-paper
take the watercooler
I'm so anti-it I can't put it into words
there's a kind of wave bye bye
that never really happens

that is just ongoing –
like saying all the time the whole party
I need to go soon I need to go soon
and people keep offering you stuff and
telling you stories
we mime speech bubbles
we suck our thumbs
indulgence is desperate
I'm such a flatterer
You are all so brilliant
You've written good poems
many of you have
I want to print out all your poems
and scrunch them up
and stuff them in my clothes
maybe read them first!
just maybe / no promises
my favourite Romantic poet is
Anna Laetita Barbauld
I wear my fear around me
I fan it out on my pillow
and spray my pillow with it
I've never been moved by staff meetings
I hated *Call Me By Your Name*
except the conversation with a fish
and the clothes
the conversations with people
all through were so horrible

and then I watched it with someone who
hated it and I started to like it more
but *God's Own Country* I didn't have so
much beef with except the crouchy
wash was borrowed wholesale
from *Brokeback Mountain*
my name all of a sudden is Mark Kermode
I loved *Benjamin* and *Please Like Me*
I loved *Space Boobs in Space*
good evening to you all
it's the audience that makes a performance
you are sleeping with stuff attached to you
you are car-less and sometimes annoying
but I don't hold that against you

**Apple Poem**

I met a potter
and her t-shirt
said "waste my time"
like a dare

someone behind me:
"it's going to be
a simple, authentic
documentary"

sand all
over my legs in
particles

and cans
of Lemon
under the surface

I soured the cherries
for this Hungarian soup
at home myself
with a look

because

nobody knows

how to
bite me
right

## Midsummer Wet Dream / Soggy Nightmare

I led us all in a Pool-ympics and
there was the underwater sprint, the freestyle jump,
the freestyle handstand and the 4 width breast stroke.

Me and you and you formed a synchronized swimming
troupe – The RSC (after our initials) and debuted
our new show, called the title of this poem.

The moves are basic. We're kind of minimalist
in our choreography. We wave to the left,
wave to the right, then back to the left.
At this point, we sort of sit back into the pool
and raise our right leg, then our left.
After that, we turn to our right and open
our arms akimbo, then we put them
up into a diving position and spin 180 °
we peel off sideways into the water
one by one. After that, we get back to our feet,
lie on our backs. We spin over one by one
and finish with this huge flourish, popping
out the water like dolphins looking for a ball
and an audience.

DM me for the video, it's really something.

**When I eat yoghurt**

I don't use a spoon
I fold the foil top into a scoop
À la Poul Gernes
I drizzle honey oh I drizzle honey
I keep the drizzle coming all week long
The last bit of the yoghurt I let get crusted
When I choose a colour I choose a pastel colour or two
When I drink a drink I like it very fruity or very
    vegetably
I like flowers that look like people
I actually prefer a mousse
I fantasise about poetry readings in dentist's waiting
    rooms
I like dentists because a dentist once told me
I had a beautiful smile and didn't need braces
Fromage Frais is a-ok
I do need braces though just not on my teeth
The crusted yoghurt is gross but amazing at the same
    time
I want someone else to write poems but them to be my
    poems
I'd be ok with our poems
Just
I was like oh no seriously I definitely need braces
I like dentists because they give you a pink mouthwash
I always say: oh yes I'll taste the *Rosé* no problem

And because their equipment is so torturous but they're
 so sweet usually
I wanted/want the metallic taste and I wanted to have
 something
To fool around with with my tongue
Recreational braces we could call them
The pasta art of dentistry
I like dentists because they put plastic gloves on their
 hands
And make you stretch your jaw ways you didn't know
 you could
And because they have posters of teeth

**Colonoscopy**

I don't know any answers
aero bars enduro
shifter sounds like cycling
or gymnastics let's go with
weight lifting I call a lot of
ambulances me and ripped
jeans, the word pals.
In the middle seat people's
elbows touch my middle.
I want a colonoscopy
is it possible to book one
for pleasure
a fantasy where I meet a guy called
Something Oscopi
and I take his name
we get married like we're living
in the 19th Century because
that's traditional
and my name becomes
Colin Oscopi
Beats headphones
was Merrill Streep in R*endition*
what's the name of the one
with Helen Mirren about drones?
I define my sexuality like if I
could choose to be Luigi Galvani

or Lucia Galvani or the frog
I'd choose to be the frog
and I'd date frogs
my frog muscles twitching
everyone I know is writing
Scottish Poetry
with biological charge
make me write a poem
make me write an essay
yeah just try to make me
I put that line in there just now
said the fisherperson
to the fish
someone once told me
that if you halve tomatoes
and squeeze them a little
and rub them all over your body
that it
has some benefit
for me
or for the tomatoes
or whoever eats the tomatoes
I'm croaking from the pulpit
how much would that cost
all seedy
and heavier than air

*Reifying Desire 3*, Jacolby Satterwhite (2013)


        there
       are parts
      of my body I'd need a map to find
      but they can be seen from the space station

a hoax ok

        like hygiene if we meet make it the friday
          sound-


                    track
                 by ghouls
              bubbles streaming
              from my breasts
              before me
                salt and cleaning


        planned
        to meet
        that way
          it never happened
        the way
        I make
        a baby

is to be
a baby
the way

                         I make
                   a T-Cell is to eat
                  more doughnuts
                    than I can bear
                     I have this

  dream
  T in this
  instance not
Testosterone

                   *Oh Boy* by Buddy Holly
               sometimes I feel the word fur
             being whispered when I walk
            and I whisper back something lovely
     because I'm not one to argue
      cool the semi-precious ease
        breath down my neck
          these are the things that'll happen
            if I don't comply
              with your demands for let them eat / me /

and you really
   mean you
     eat cautiously
slamming on your brakes
like a Porsche and speed gun
meeting

**It's very early**

we're up watching
your phone to see
if we need to book
a taxi to the hospital
for our dearest friend
and then I unfairly accuse
you of stealing all the covers
and you ask me to roll over
Dumbo (affectionately)
and then your breathing
changes and I go downstairs
to make myself coffee
and a cheeky can't-believe-
I-just-said-that Fruit & Fibre
and when I get back we
still haven't heard anything.

## Epistemo-erotic Advantage

Kind of faint
texture of chamois
feeling reedy
stuffed, I make a fine ornament
mallard
high on a shelf
I said before about trying to act the husband
all I'm as dry as a piece of bread
but a dick has a metallic sheen
in this poem in a newspaper
I once had a coffee in a coffee shop
called Café Fat Man
I jumped out of my skin
coffee capsule
dawn breaks
antipasto
the bit I find confusing is how
come I
get bitten by desire and
I bite desire and I desire to bite
I was myself with a flannel
I was glued to the spot
the concept in science of the pseudobulge
Mr The Heron by Giorgio Bassani
Mr Wheat that springeth green
a shoestring

sounded corny and inchoate
chewing gum
I found out a strange
family secret
You're such a hairy cat
I found out a really peculiar circumstance
You want me to tell you
and I already told you

**Definitely wear trainers!**

If everywhere was like Kenny Scharf's
*Cosmic Cavern Closet*, or better yet that we
didn't just glow in the dark but that we
actually changed shape, moulded like gum
to someone's shoe or someone's b-u-m.
I'm in this strange mood because
If anyone really cared
Oh I just can't get Up Helly Aa
out my head
I love a bar with dewdrops on the walls
I love a dewdrop on the forehead
Dewdrops in general are most satisfactory
a yellow dog made out
of bubble gum and it is the
exact opposite of Jeff Koons
the difference between blue tack and selotape is…
feels that way to me
serotype is a whole different sphere
I wish everywhere hubba'd + bubba'd
And everyone glopped and gushed
meant I could sink into {TBC}
meant I could be a part of
everyone treats you mean until
you let down their guard for them
and you do that by making a fool
of yourself but if you make too much

of a fool of yourself people start being mean again
{Continued} and you know what happens
to bubbles right?
They ju-ust flo-oat a-wa-y.

**Your Barking Lesson**

I want you to have a good time
Do you get tired of my athletic hauteur?
Beginners to the left
Adventurous to the right
Experts in the middle

Rearrange yourselves
At the first growl
Of this tambourine

Using a burger bun as some
kind of phone

I'm going to call your parents
And tell them how good you are
at barking

**Mozartian**

The smell of brick walls
rain wiping its bum against
moss, dopey guys drooling
over jeans, drool – oh
so grownup but part of
who I am. I want new
flavours. I'm mad about
Fanta.

TV, breakfast cereal,
nets full of balloons and
inflatables. Thought
Inflatable was a name
like Isabel.

The wonderful thing is
inflatable is relative.
Soapbubbles get me high.
I want to be more brave
but I think bravery's actually
really stupid.

**Imprint**
*after Anna de Noailles*

I sit on life
with a squeeze and a pressure
until I can't tell when I get up
whether it's me
or the day that's got so hot
and sweet-sour

The sea's cheek-spread,
bicarb of soda whisper,
turbulent gurgle / gag
taste to me a little like me

In a wooded area I'm always on edge
if it's a hilltop I sway in gusts
and also shrink into pimples, heather
bristles / bruises all of which get me going

Maybe fields are more me- especially
ditches - the teem! - buzzed with
bees and flowers where it feels like something
is giving birth to me eating mud and buttercups
and loving it or not hating it

I don't know whether they're the same
what life is and what I am but whenever
I'm gloomy af life feels gloomy af to me

**Kissed by Bubbles**

Via a conversation with the brilliant poet
Erin Gannon, I found out about
Bubbles, persona of Anthony Torres,
from San Francisco, who was shot dead
in The Tenderloin in September 2017.
Bubbles was a House DJ, artist and activist,
whose work included Tranny Snow Cones,
churned out on the street from an
Italian Ice Cream Machine.

Bubbles pasted their tag all over the city,
a self-portrait with text saying:
*shut up and dance.*

Bubbles was a regular
(like the opposite of a fixture) at a dance night called
Housepitality. In a video for *The City Exposed*
by Mike Kepka in 2012, Bubbles said:
"Friends say that Bubbles is the fun me but
Bubbles is just like a character that I like to
go out as. It's fun. Bubbles is more like a toy.
... Bubbles is just Bubbles.
I feel empowered. The attention
is nice, I'm an attention whore, it
makes me feel important and loved..."

Bubbles' wardrobe included 60s flower print dresses,
ski goggles, long blond wigs (dreads, Heidi braids,
pig tails, Marilyn waves, Dusty Springfield hive,
you name it), shocking pink glasses,
shocking pink bra, bright yellow belt,
fade-change purple wig, polka bows,
denim jacket, multi-colour swimming
costume, multi-colour platform shoes,
hoop earrings, spangly studded hat,
Smiths T-Shirt, Red Nose, Joy Division T Shirt,
Rolling Stones T Shirt, hoop earrings,
pink animal print handbag, purple and white
striped bikini, wobbly eye specs, cloud Y Fronts,
Mariachi hat, a pink phone,
silver hot pants,
space helmet, love heart sun glasses, beads, pearls,
tight blue jeans, fluffy pastel cardigan, huge blue
and fluorescent pink boots, silver and black swirl
leggings, black and white check prom dress,
tights in an array of colours and an
"The Artist is Broke" sweatshirt…

Bubbles ran a night called Sissy Bar.

One of Bubbles's artworks was a mixed media of
Marilyn Monroe blowing bubble gum.

Another of Bubbles' tag lines was

"Not the kind you blow. But you never know"
One of Bubbles' works is a Polaroid of them on a bed
with a mirror and underneath it says,
(very Magritte / very Mondrian / very Bas Jan Ader
if you ask me):
"This is Not a Line"

What I love about what I've seen of Bubbles'
art, and the way they spoke about it is
it's all fancy, all surface : no concept. The work
is strange, idiosyncratic, and
it refuses to solidify, refuses to singularize.

There are pictures of Bubbles made into digital mosaics
and all of Bubbles' work seems like
self portraiture as bubble-mosaic.
Bubbles like a lo-fi Akihiro Miwa.

There's a video on Youtube of Bubbles dancing at
a night called Stretch Sundays, at one point getting
down
to do a kind of assisted shoulder stand
(hand stand-esque with someone holding their legs
in the air) and then they do some sexy press ups.

Talk-singing over a piece of music
released by Will Flat, Bubbles says: "I'm holding on
for dear life to San Francisco, the sub culture

they're trying to get rid of, it's still here..."
and

"there were clubs that used to open Thursday through
to Monday and on Monday the night was called Rehab"

and

"I used to get chased by the cops all the
time because of what I
was doing all the time"

Bubbles' Instagram is gorgeous.

There's a Barbie doll with Bubbles' handlebar
    moustache,
pictures of Bubbles with a "Frenchie from my flight
    home",
beautiful digital drawings in black ink,
posters for club nights, headdress pics, bulge pics,
boob pics, collages, anti-Nazi posters, outfits outfits
outfits, collages, berets, leather jackets, leggings,
lots of barbies, a nun filling up the screen wash of
a 4 x 4, masks, tights, a Miss Talent Sash, sun glasses,
shoes, loads of museum pop art, loads of homemade
pop art, sassy leg-crosses, early on a note saying "I
    would never
be a part of anything. I would never really belong

anywhere, and I knew it, and all my life would be
the same, trying to belong, and failing. Always
something would go wrong. I am a stranger and I
always will be, and after all I didn't really care",
Simpson's nail art, this whole series of pictures
of people on the street posing with the pink telephone,
its wire stretching out of the frame, lots of fags slipped
dangling out of Bubbles' mouth, a strange BMX phase,
and just so much more.

Bubbles' art is also all the tourist snapshots
of them in the streets, which must be diffuse,
lost, deleted. Bubbles grins or pouts in every one.
Bubbles hit local news in 2016 when they got ejected
    from a
bar because the bartender said the manager didn't like
    the
way they looked. In the SF Examiner, a friend says
"if Bubbles came to your party, you knew it was a
    fucking good party"

Bubbles would set up impromptu Street discos with pop
    corn
as a kind of civic aesthetic duty… Paranoid London,
    who were
due to collaborate with Bubbles, have released a tribute
    EP,

*The Boombox Affair* which uses vocals from a Facebook
    post
Bubbles made of breaking into a construction yard and
    holding
a solo rave. The track 'Beats and Bubbles' begins:
"This is what I brought and I'm playing my own
records!"

The choice of Bubbles as a name seems utterly
perfect and utterly devastating - amorphous,
conjoining, beautiful, strange, surface….also
fragile and defiant to the max.

I get more from Bubbles'
insta than I do from *Spherologies*.

One artwork by Bubbles is a mirror written on
with pink and blue lipstick that says:

"you've been

kissed by Bubbles".

**Hi Mum I'm in a Poem, Just…**

So and so anticipated such and such
problem we're facing today
I've been looking into organic burial pods
I'd like to be turned into a cocoa bean
or some gym equipment
please do not bin the superglue
you know the word teacak'd
maybe we need more salt
excessive virtuosity
is forgivable
the bees knees
ache don't drip
I'd like to be encrusted
Michael Bublé playing in some kind of non-chapel
ceremony
or just exploded e.g. cancelled
like some desperate
scandal

**Softness**

Bhupen Khakhar's
*Two Men at Banaras*
my favourite painting
today

stony salt mounds
fleshy beach
velvet ribbon

buttock and moob architecture

and one man with grey
hair propped up
by another man
who needs no
propping up!

## *Zebra and Parachute*, Christopher Wood

such an aisle!
somebody, please,
cough to fill the space

protractor yawn
gold dung
penitent questions
funny mallow
foam

now I know
(thought bubble)
it reminds me of
that guy on the plane

with no conception of space or touch
legs wide; elbow very close
the first person to cough
wins a twirl

which is a confection
kind of like a flake

**So many poems**

I write so many poems, sometimes
I think it's going to do me some harm
Me to poets
Airport massage chair to masseurs
I was going to be even more dramatic
But my main thing is saying it
So as to not have it said against me
There's a lot that can be a poem
I keep saying that
It's a new tic
There are so many poems I love
Sometimes I think the number of poems
I love is just about Instagram but it isn't
I did a workshop for some interpreters
I started on this rant about what I thought
a work of art was. Tom Leonard was in there
more than once. June Jordan too. Beverly
Dahlen. The funny part about it was the
interpreters were not meant to be too
interested in the content of what I was saying
just the language and then the next day,
I wasn't privy to this part, they
talked about the expressions I used and my
Rhetoric. I did my best. I started the talk
by saying: "who has Latin?" sort of like a
Grindr refresh, and then fell about laughing.

**Landing**

We're a big orange baby in the clouds
Mwah mwah hiccup and woopsie
Next to me's shoeless - okish feet

I won't say patchwork
Hedgerows hastily stapled in
60 Minute Makeover
Slicing harnesses

Wordsworth:

"Hedgerows, somebody get me the fucking hedgerows...

Hello? I need some hedgerows over here

Like ten minutes ago!"

**I can't do it alone, want to join in?**
*after Poul Gernes - 'I can't do it alone, want to join in?'*
*and also after Alison Knowles - 'Make a Salad'*

I was going to say tweet me your favourite words
and I mean I'm not going to say don't
but most of all send poems
I love reading poems
they don't even have to be good
what does good mean when it's about
language use which we all do all the time
poetry is like speed-walking
you don't actually have to even send them to me
if you don't want to
just write them
and read them and think to yourself
hm, I like that word
hm, I love that word
those two together they are so delicious
so strange so scary so tempting so awful
etc etc etc etc
you get the picture – I mean poem!

**The word unputdownable**
*after reading Niviaq Korneliussen's Crimson*

tastes so racy and ace
this is a book I love
whenever I hear the phrase our very own
when someone carries a torch
it's only a matter of time
before they torch a car
Sometimes I eat bananas
Sometimes I dress myself
Hair repels and fodder attracts
The polite way of putting it
I'm buying more than one copy
I'm designing an outfit with a bull bar
and a beak
I'm going to wear it
with a banana shirt
just to confuse my students
I have this other weird plan
where I get myself a job interview
and just say "No comment"
to every question
I saw a boy who looked
fourteen with a huge gash on
his leg hobbling around Queen St
station and he refused all help

I actually love chiller cabinets
I don't scream "Bucolic!"

**My new friend has a bathtub**

the shape of a cashew
and a stain
on his living room carpet

I tried to make it better
and made it worse

The tap is either much too hot
or Evian-cold

and I like to be in the bath
while it runs -
my mildest kink

I love the torrent
and being in an increasing
volatile body

*Somebody* doesn't put bubble bath out

When I dunk my head I get the drift
oxi-action is almost meaningless
and my nose starts to sting

The water drains with
sucky sinking pressure

and a slapping sound
*I'm a diplomat; I'm a diplomat*

The towel is frogspawn-patterned

He's laid out a banana and juice

It only *looks* worse

Just have patience
naughty one

**Thorn Bug Huff-Song**

I'm spiky
and not just by email

I burst bubbles
in my sleep

I'm backwards-coming-forwards
camouflage green

I'm difficult
to spot

and difficult to chew.

It's kind of an act

I love sap more than I can say
and this is my thorny secret:

I'm just a sugary mess

## *Bubbles Galore* (1996), dir. Cynthia Roberts

Cynthia Roberts is an underrated
filmmaker whose work includes
*The Last Supper* (1994) which is about
a dinner party when someone knows
they're about to die. *Bubbles Galore*
(1996) is a very weird feminist sex movie
starring Nina Hartley, Tracy Wright,
Daniel MacIvor and Annie Sprinkles
that was controversial because it was
funded in part through Canadian
government arts funding. One irate
reviewer online says it "presents a
world where God is a hideous,
sex-crazed exhibitionist" and plenty
of people call it the worst movie
they have ever seen. A lot of people
describe the acting as unconvincing.
Which, for what it's worth, is my favourite
kind of acting.

The opening credits feature what looks
like ultra close-ups of a Christmas tree,
with its red and green baubles, and
every so often a floating cut-and-pasted
naked body. Some of the first words

of the film are "Joy to the world, the
Lord has come".

Bubbles Galore the character is a gifted
star-turned-porn-director, under pressure
from her producer. At one point Bubbles' Ex,
rival director Godfrey Montana, says he
has something Bubbles wants and Bubbles
has something he wants. Bubbles replies
that she can't think what in the world
she could want from him. He says "clout.
Clout is what I got". Clout versus Bubbles.
Bubbles will always win. But to try
and convince her even more he says "You
and me, we're different. We've got class.
We've got class coming out of our assholes".
When Bubbles manages to resist this charm,
he vows to take her down. I feel like I want to
re-write that bit of dialogue replacing "class"
with "bubbles".

God, played by an Ariel-like Annie Sprinkles,
sees all this and starts to meddle, sending new
talent in the form of a virgin called Dory, to
Bubbles' door. It's like in Jack Smith's story
'Normal Love': "God's plump buns rested serenely
on the ziricorn and rhinestone throne". Bubbles

shares with her assistant Viv her desire, I think
she says dream, to make a triple X film that
everyone – gay, straight, married, single,
all over the world, will enjoy. "Not just a
bunch of raincoats" is how she puts it.

Bubbles teaches Dory how to have sex,
asks Viv to go home and when Viv comes
back the next day she's pissed because
Bubbles and Dory have got carried away.
Viv reminds Bubbles she needs to get ready
for an interview with a journalist so she showers
and it is during their awkward conversation
alone that Viv says to Dory:
"Listen Kid, nobody works with Bubbles.
Everybody works for Bubbles."

While Bubbles is interviewed, Dory has a
bath, and spreads bathbubbles out over her
body. Meanwhile, Buck, an old flame of
Bubbles, who she's already helped out with cash
gets a visit from two of Godfrey's henchmen,
who force him to make a call to Bubbles
taking her up on the offer of a job, with
the ulterior motive of sabotaging the film
by stealing the negative.

Bubbles' film looks amazing. It's very dream-like
and foamy, of course: inflatables, whipped cream
I think, neon lights and a guy bouncing up and
down. There's someone in a fluffy pig outfit
and Bubbles at one point wears this fab red
cat suit with weird sausage-like antenna. They
are all laughing while the make the film.

Buck refuses to screw Bubbles over and Godfrey
goes nuts. Viv declares her love for Bubbles and
her jealousy over Dory. There's a weird fight scene
in an icy car park between Buck, Godfrey and his
muscle, which plays out while Bubbles and Viv
have sex. The fight culminates in Godfrey and
the henchmen firing on and wounding Buck as
he lopes into some scrubland. There's a Canadian
flag and the CN Tower in the distance. Buck finds
a phone box and calls Bubbles, who drops what
she's doing (making love to Viv) and dashes
to his rescue.

Buck confesses the deal he made with Godfrey,
which alerts Bubbles that Viv is most likely in
danger. Godfrey notices Dory on the screen
and tries to get Viv to tell him her name,
which she refuses to do, but one of the muscle

finds her name and address in Bubbles' office.

Godfrey orders them to find Dory and bring
her back to Bubbles' apartment. When they
get to her address, it's a church. "Hey, she lives
in a church!" Bubbles races back, and finds
Godfrey (in the hat of the red cat suit) and
Viv (tied up and gagged.) He taunts Bubbles
until Dory and the muscle arrive back.

Dory whispers to the girls that she doesn't
have time to explain but that everything
is going to be fine because she has some fairy
dust. When Godfrey tries it with her she sprinkles
it all over and it's like fireworks going off in
the place. The fairy dust actually seems like bubbles
from a wand and Dory is going wild with it.
You see Annie Sprinkles aka God huffing
and puffing towards them from above. Godfrey
is trying to attack Bubbles but Bubbles and Dory
get the upper hand.

Godfrey who along with his henchmen seems
to have vanished is next seen on a lead with
lots of angels or demons whipping him and
laughing.

Dory it turns out is Bubbles' Guardian Angel,
whose job on earth is to make it a safe place for
all sex workers. At the end of the film, they finish
making the film and it does really well at the
what do you call it box office.

**Fudge Packer**

Flirtation is not capitalism
I don't need to tell *you* that but
I always spread the icing thickly
I have this illusion
there are people employed to
unspread my enthusiasm
to excavate the middle sixteen layers
Tons and tons of water and sugar
(the stuff of love!)
goes into making this confection
My department is mainly cellophane,
ribbon and sticky stuff
It should be fancy but not fancy fancy
It should be out of the everyday
Fruit and nuts fruit and nuts even I get exhausted
Someone once called me fiercely gauche (I think)
People who have travelled away suddenly look
glowing and gorgeous like they only get out of
bed for a pina colada
I'm not sure I totally get the everyday
I always want to ice my spatial stories!
A city is like a bar of fudge to me
My department is surface aesthetics
Not so far out of the everyday that you wouldn't want it
Not so beyond the pale as to be out of reach

There's an exception to the people who have gone away
    thing
Flirtation is a jelly bean pressed into
Whenever I finish one I look at it
and feel like my friend's dad walking in on me
in a white sheet murmuring "I'm a nun"
I talk fancy because it's becoming
Saying "your voice is well your voice has this
Elevation, like a vantage point"
I have a streak in me that must
Always want to be in a pickle

**after *Bully and Bitch*, Asim Butt (2008)**

In 2003 the artist Asim Butt
made two murals in the grounds of
a shrine to the Sufi Mystic
Abdullah Shah Ghazi in Karachi.
One was called *5 Ways to Kill a Man*,
after the poem by Edwin Brock,
and it was about the Shock & Awe
policy in the Iraq War. The other
was about glue-sniffing, and featured
children he met when he was working
on the first mural. The shrine to
Abdullah Shah Ghazi provides two
meals daily to those in need. It's a
hub and refuge for homeless, queers,
transsexuals, drug addicts. The shrine was attacked
by suicide bombers in 2010, killing 10,
but operates again. Asim Butt died the same year.
Abdullah Shah Ghazi was murdered in a forest.
Asim Butt has a painting called *Bully and Bitch*,
of three dogs and a bunch of cars. Two of the dogs,
one butch and one slight, are staring each other
down while there's another butch dog looking
the other way. The wheels on the parked cars
are at weird angles.

## Hesitation Cocktail

Does anyone have experience of a trapped nerve?
I think I have one in my tongue.
It's not painful, just inconvenient.
If you pressed me I'd say a gooey dogged numbness.
I have an appointment with the Dr next week
but I'd rather find some solution myself.
My hobby-business loans stemware for
Coming Out Parties - our slogan -
Nothing Shattered Except Heteronormativity!
I audition for TV shows but never get them.
I told a producer:
I'm not sure I *really needed* that cup of tea.
Do they still manufacture these ingredients?
Lemon Juice, Canadian Club, Swedish Punch?
I'd rather be reading *Some Tame Gazelle*.
Business is sluggish. People are sloppy.
And I haven't even thought about a garnish.

**Hint hint**

Sweet pea you are filthy
the same tea towel for
plates and pots
just leave it and I'll sort it later
I like to move them around on a tray
4 in a bed's on and somebody just licked
the sink
Don't get me started on your armpits
or forever hold your tongue
I'm no parsleyphobe
your knuckles are pink dolphins
chomping through that water
but sweet pea you are filthy
there's nowhere this poem can go
I'll dry; you wash
I don't mean the dishes

### Email me tomorrow morning or else

Was my tone ok? I was going for something
Dom-but-kitsch. Steed-like. Blossoming
in the art. I'm like *I'm a task master.*
*I'm such a task master*. Don't tell, don't get. I used
to think poetry was really easy then I figured
it was me that was really easy. I get
myself tangled but there's always a way through
the kink. I used to write all my poems in the voice
of a cash fag - grovelling and apologetic - giving
myself a hard time - but I'm
having a go at switching it up. Shouldn't have
suffered that hesitation, still getting the hang.
The trigger was Deliveroo bringing Pepsi instead
of Max. I was drooling and disappointed, like
when the Arts Council make some really
unfathomable choice. The emailee in question's
a new PT I'm fluttering about, with a view
to knocking this here pulpy banana bread
back into its loaf tin. And the reply came back
sharpish: ok keen bean, with a bicep emoji.

**My car is an unreliable narrator**

And a sadist re: its fuel dial
Oh for somebody who knows
How to talk calmly to a machine!
I just went to Daniel Kitson
It was really funny
I'm walking home - from whence
I've had a number of missives aka texts
I stand outside a Card Factory
The shelves are almost empty
A charity shop display of blue glass
And a dress that I'd love to say
I used to have a pair of curtains like
But I still do
A copy of *Zos Speaks* by Austin Osman Spare
Green and gold and £70
This is still the shop window
I want to read *Myrmecophile*
By Ifti Nasim, the poet who
Was also a car sales person
And who would retort
When someone asked how big
An engine was "why? Are you
Intending to sleep with it?"
It's way passed my bed time
If I could read poetry all day
And I'm not a million miles away

I'd buy a watch with an inbuilt camera from duty free
And just be the asshole who solves the mystery of desire

**My Humiliation Fetish**

We listen to Nakhane all night and all morning.
We hire some kind of open top car.
Turtle Wax it.
At a push we open all the windows and the sun roof
of a regular car.
You drive me to a golf course.
Deranged, manicured lawns. Hanging Baskets
with nasturtiums and dahlias.
Really quiet and tranquil and corduroy.
You park up as close to one of the greens as possible.
I'm wearing hardly a thing except
golf shoes and cap and a tee between my teeth.
First we sit a while just watching the comings
and goings, the buggies, and listening to the clack of
irons and the buzzed out chatter, and coins in pockets,
And then you just put your fist on the car horn
and refuse to let go.

## A wrapper

It was crucial as anything
that we wore surgical masks and
blue plastic gloves and orange plastic
aprons before we opened the door
and went in to your isolation for
three ritualistic masked
bumps on the cheek and muffled
surgical kissing noises.

It was crucial as anything and then
one day they ran out of masks
and told us we'd probably be
alright as long as you didn't cough.

You were under the impression that
the masks etc were to protect
you from us, because in your condition
you were weak, but we were under
the impression it was the other way around.

We risked it, under medical encouragement,
surprising the kind of daring glee. "We've all
been doing it", they giggled, without the masks,
just aprons and gloves.
The way we shuffled in, I took
the seat over by the window, and Reuben

the seat by the bed. You coughed a few times
and we brushed it off, tiny little inward winces.
We spoke about holidays we'd have when they
let you out, and bottles of wine we'd stashed
in your fridge, along with a Cornish Tickler,
to which you said "yes please" and the souped-
up Uber we came in, with gaming tables and
massage function. We spoke about the food
and about what the Drs had most recently said
and about the view from the window into
an adjacent block of the hospital. On the plane home
we started feeling a tickle in our sinuses and then
our ears popped and it's three weeks now and
they haven't unpopped.

**Weird Fight**

My trousers were clumped
You asked if the fly was down
I said no
Then you went bananas

## Sir Walter Scott
*after a conversation with Jane Goldman*

The thing about Scott is:
he's unquotable, un-pick-up-able,
and I'm not just being mean, the way up
the monument is closed, it's all in the
demanding flatness, the grandiose sweep,
the unreality, the *woodenness* of the heroism,
which I try to love and embrace,
both in the sense of taking part and
locking in the tight, BO bear hug
of a *drab, necessary progress*, as useful
as the g in lasagne, i.e. a little, a fleck
of use. Progress is mythic,
I get that, one of those myths you only pull
away from when you've got yourself hooked
on some other idea. Liberty, spontaneity,
flexibility, poetry, community, camp, artifice,
homographesis even, and not to get all
romantic novelist on you, but, revenge,
overcooked and left to refrigerate in Edinburgh,
or love, even love, which *rules the court,
and the grove*. In my barely-getting-started
experience and limited knowledge,
it's harder than it looks to love
someone who's a Sir, with a monstrous-
monument to them, a totem to them, fact;

harder to, or easier not to, or better for the environment, I forget which.

## A Famous Singer's Mother

I'm never having children but if
I were to, and there were two of them,
I'd call them Lore and Apocrypha.
Swaying about our kitchen,
Me and Mr Me (though we'd
not in a million years get married),
would laugh and say, *well, if you believe Lore,
this…*, and *if you believe Apocrypha, that…*

and they'd chatter exasperatingly away,
weird obsessive stories about a famous singer's
mother, who apparently said that whenever
he read aloud, it could be anything at all,
some fan mail, an invitation card, a phone bill,
some maths prep, the back of a microwave packet,

she all of a sudden felt a chill across her
shoulder blades and goose pimples on her neck
and wrists, like someone who just discovered
the Hot Dudes Reading Instagram account,
and opened the window to cool off. *Spooky*,
I'd think, and blush.

**Punching Time**

I don't actually believe he's not doing art.
Whenever we start cooking you say:
I'm in the driver's seat
The weather's more exciting than "Love Nests".
Every baby's entitled to sound, egg tempera teeth
and the way David Martin paints Muslin!
Every noob, a sweeting apple.
I want you to take a picture of me like
Carl Van Vechten of Paul Cadmus.
Angular and geeky, steely background,
gawky gaze (say *yes the fleet's in*).
Imagine writing a dissertation with no
delete button!
I dreamt that a child bust out of me
and said *you think you're so cool;*
*I'm here to make you suck.*
*And it's a pleasure to make your*
*acquaintance.*
In a crisp tone.
*I donated my hair for charity.*

**As Much As I love It
Sometimes It Makes Me Sick**

You are finishing a glass of wine
I'm eating Trolli sour worms
the tv talk-sings whisperato
we have to get up at 5
yesterday a father cut his arm
the sea's discarded cummerbund
when stressed
strawberry shortcake is a starter
and when not I can't remember
I'm so shit at money stuff
that worms are sour doesn't surprise me
we sometimes sleep in shifts
submissions submissions
google: how to make something zing?
your cough is kind of sumptuous
we have really beautiful duvet covers
it's our thing and it keeps us safe
from Macho demons

**Rome was not like you see in the movies**

It was all goldfish swimming together in tea cups
and the sentence *everybody should have a fake show biz hello*

on everyone's lips, the mean nothing,
inflatable drinks holders bobbing together
in a swimming pool
I want my clothes to match my desires and I want
A body that makes sense in the glimmer

I want to use the phrase "mortal critter" in a sonnet
I wish I could secure great publishing deals for students
I feel like we're swimming pools swimming together in space
Not to have watched all of "Please Like Me" this weekend

We argue so often I don't know what to do with myself
We're getting younger, glossier, bloodier and more prone to crying
My desires outweigh my ideas and my beliefs.

**Raw and Boiled Tongue**
*my attempt at Mujun after Abū Nuwās*

Hi, cable that leads straight from the fridge
to mucocutaneous junctions.

Somebody once asked to put
part of him in my juicer, back
when I had a juice blog that got more
than two hits a month.

He was being playful and I took the
bait but the plan never came to
what's another word for fruition?

This is a painted window-stunned
dove. And on the underside it
says "ow, ouch, yes".

We listened to Kath Bloom, that was
how we linked up, fitted together.

We fell asleep really easily, like two little
drugged animals brought home from the vet.

My coffee table was lacquered like one of Asger Jorn's
Luxury Paintings. Covered with string. From all the
parcels.

He sent me these Ruin Your Week Packages that I wouldn't
recommend to anyone but it's free to say thank-you, so I did.

Mustard on toast, he fed me. Sharpie, in a Twombly scrawl,
all over my, all over me.

The cable zinged an X-Ray spasm, Tchelitchew,
it made DIY noises in the night, and us in its buzz,
best of friends, we had a zealous perversion,
a Dodo-May-Care attitude, that protected us from trouble.

Still, even I balked at the raw and boiled tongue.
I guess I found my limit, I said.

## Our Light and Our Fan

They're connected
And the fan makes this high pitched rattle
We call it the mad turkey

I leave the light off at 6am and use the torch on my
phone
And my body looks dappled, waxed, a bit-too-porny
like it's covered in ice

I want to be more of a poet than I am
I'm such a silly sausage

People are weird and selfish and love themselves
People are nice and kind and want to be around you
I used to be so freaky about poems being messages
Like poems are more than messages
But poems can be messages and the message can be
Sensuous but evanescent

Something like

I had a childhood dream to have a dog chase me down
the street
Don't make me yelp at you

**Two sweaters for one person**
**or one sweater for more than one**
after Muriel Spark's *Territorial Rights*

I want to fit more of myself in
myself. Enormous-headed flowers
that look like you could book
a holiday with them, or exchange
some leftover currency, or head up
a citizen's advice bureau, or
download a recipe for something
zero fat, zero effort. Nobody's going
to know what hit them with this poem.
Because it won't hit them. Maybe build
slowly, like the pressure of a huge
trainer collection, always
there, in a cupboard and overflow box
chastising, gloating, goading you for
wearing anything less than charismatic.
Bare foot tip toe to the fridge, please-uh.
*I'm not in rivalry never with no-one.*
I cancelled my sky subscription because
I never watched it. There's room in here,
just unvelcro, unhoodie, pop the rubber
air bubble in your maxes, just allow your
comfort quota to dip a little, to soak up,
quiver, ooze, burst and sink.

**TV Hairline Perk**

Hi, Pink Traveler
in Leith. Park, rev,
perkier van hilt;
a river knelt, hip!

Link heart, VIP, re-
vealin pith, k. Err,
hankie, err (TV lip):
rap their Kelvin.

Ah, help! Rev in irk-
pearl hike, RVT,
pavin' the RR, like
rethink Rev-A-Lip.

Her interval.  Kip.

Thinker, prevail,
privet ink, harken
vainer p-kilt, her
pink veil. Rather.

Arrive, knit, help,
preen viral kith.
Printer ilk. Have
a think, revel, rip,

rip, Navel Hiker,
ken, thrivin' pearl,
rave lither pink,
think Earl Viper,

Earl Thriven-Pink.
Thank Lire! Viper!
Heal ink trip, reveal River Nth Kip.

## Meadowbank Changing Manifesto

We need another word
for badminton. If everyone's
comfortable calling squash
squash, at least for the meantime,
we should consider the following
suggestions: swish, jumpwhack,
trainersqueek shimmyracket,
weirdsport, hurrystyles, nothockey,
ritzyexuberance, breathybeats,
SmashThePants, thintennis,
whichsideamimeanttobeongame,
whatsthescorenowsport,
high-and-fluttery, middlerackety,
deftness, highnet, shuttlecockhitting,
over-the-top, sullyknee, pinstrip,
or how about we play it really
cautious and classy and just
trim the word to BAD? We'll take
a vote so it should be pretty
painless. Starting localised
in this sweaty, noise-art
cardboard changing room,
but branching out like a
brakeless shuttlecock that's
been watching Forrest Gump,
we're going to refashion

every sport until the world's
a different and/or better place!

## Nice Honk, Van Driver

Deep down you know it's me
I'm all over this like a rash
I'm holding a little model
of a van and you're inside it
think I'm kidding
the jumper I'm wearing feels
so alive, I feel like adding on
a service charge for keeping
me warm and zippy today your
Honk made my day sweetheart
like a magazine rejection (which
is secretly why I'm in this game)
I just love being teased
and anyway after this I'll come
home and my lamps, Metaxa-copper
as they warm up to illuminate
a wardrobe in which I have
a shirt with peaches all over it
and a Keith Haring tracksuit
honk at those pretty please
with a watermelon on top

**after an image of Kaarlo Sarkia**

day-glo iphone screen
rotten branches
tilted – insta – are you
with me? – the guy's
chest and back -

"drenched the bathmat
with sun!"

poetry's a golden shower
a screenwash of goo

**My Mystical Love Poetry**
*for Jane Goldman*

Shams-i-Tabrīzī is
a woman & we go jogging
 - almost a whirl – got
up like Beau Tibbs
("a fine body of voice") in
gold trainers & she tells
me to read Claire Colebrook
harder & Elizabeth Grosz
again & talks to me about
*The Waves* & points out
lost dogs called Lola
& live dogs – all 19 of them -
& teaches me & all the time
while we're jogging we
have brims in our tails,
our nattiness fading in
sunny scurries, violet whorls.
We call our friends & ask them
to facetime us poems that
makes us mystical eyed &
briny & we're on a very
noisy bridge across a
motorway & fading fast but
not at all like the flowers of friendship
& the rest is a mystery couched in

web cam metaphors, a
leather deskchair rotating
some weird fractal dance,
& the hurtling of cyclists
& faster runners & barges
& children so watch this space.

**after Truong Tan, 'When Love Starts', 2006**

I knew I'd cave
eventually
an ecopoem
here we come
about forests
part trunk
part branch
part leaf etc
make me a cocktail
sap and spittle sour
make
me a green salad
oh make me representational
oh make me underwhelming
but gilded and hypnotic,
green and green,
I want to feel like I could
be bought from Pret!
Stacked in a humming
chiller no-one says
a-manger any more
date-stamped and
not to be discarded
lightly.

## Laplaplaplaplaplaplap Top

My love affair with my old laptop
was so intense I did a lot on this laptop
and now that it doesn't work in the way
it used to (it still has a curious way
of computing and making me compute)
we interact on a whole other plane

I wanted to give it one last special
treat so I took it for a day out and
before we left I noticed it was grimy
so I started to give it a kind of
bed wash with a lemon scented wipe
under its armpits, under its hood, into
its orifices and around its little muscles
but then I remembered that my friend
had got me some jasmine bubble bath
so I started running / drawing a bath
full of hot, piping, jasmine scented
water (we threw the baby out before
we started just fyi) and I got undressed
and this strange computer of mine was
already undressed

I lowered the computer into the water
I'm not very good at science so I
was partially nervous partially nah

no problem. I was confused, my tummy
curdling and my hair standing
on end. The computer sort of floated and
then gave this plastic boom into the siding

"Careful sweety" "careful honey" I whispered
and I myself started to get into the bath
we washed each other at one point I
kissed my own knee because I'm such a dope
it felt like we were undoing straightwashing
it felt good for us both to be flying in the
face of our own microbattles with technological
obsolescence. I also think we were grieving
for / with each other even though we weren't
in any more danger of expiring than we'd
ever been probably. I had misunderstood
some aspects of the computer's reticence
and inactivity. And I think the computer
hadn't been as good as it could've been
to communicate to me that it needed me
to see it differently to how I'd become
accustomed in order for us to continue
to have any meaningful association. This
process took on pace and momentum
while washing together and being together
in the bathtub.

Problem was we both got hooked on it.

Well I say problem but we were just having
some harmless pleasure. Our mutual appreciation
society was open for business! I thought of how
frustrated I had been when my computer
first started to refuse to function as I had
expected it to. But now I realized that
for the 8+ years I had had this laptop it had had
to endure the same frustration about me, that
all I was interested in was using the computer
in the exact way I felt I needed it at that time.
I was ignoring all of its sensory apparatus,
its affective absorptions and resistances, its
nerve system. It even tried to communicate
in dreams I think. I mean it really tried to jolt
me. I once dreamed of my laptop swathed in
a leopard's pelt and I couldn't get my head
around any of the word templates it kept
suggesting I use but I was never, up until this moment,
really with the computer. (Sorry for wallowing!)

The recycling bin of the matter is this: even as big data
and social media and coding and all that shit move us
towards human obsolescence, obsolescence is a space in
which queers (human, more than human) have a certain
kind of knack or calibre. Together we came up with
this slightly bizarre idea of going out to public toilets
around Edinburgh and washing in the sinks.

We went first to the place at the corner of the meadows.
I ran the water which gushed and spluttered like it had
hay fever. I got some bubble stuff and lathered over the
computer it was such a hot day you could have fried
   some
facon on my laptop. I cried a little tear and it sizzled.
The cold lather was refreshing for us both. There were
   people
stood awfully statuesque at the urinals. Someone was
   humming
*Viva Forever* by the Spice Girls under their breath. They
   started
talking to us. I said I was busy and needed a few minutes
   – it
didn't take long.

I started pinching myself in the open air.
The computer dried on the grass.
It was making a buzzing monotone.
A kind of purr.
I started writing in my mind a book on queer baldness
and/or back hair.
The first chapter on Foucault and the second chapter
I didn't get to before I noticed that the computer
was stirring
It made its way
back into the toilet
and after waiting on the grass in a daze

I got up to go back home and my
bum was green which was annoying but
not so annoying as to ruin my afternoon.

## Bartender

The bartender who used to work one place
now works another place - a fancier place.
In their old job they were really flirty – e.g.
they would say things like "ooh I'm worth the
wait" and "don't worry; I give good head" when
they'd pour a pint. It was kind of outrageous
and strange but I found it amusing. In their new
job they are much more straight but as soon as I
walk in they say "hello! long time no see!"
and pour a glass of sparkling wine and
say "this place can afford to give it away"
with a conspiratorial wink. They've been
encouraged to go for Cocktail contests
and they've won a prize sponsored by
Belvedere. I give them a generous tip and
on my way out I hear them say to a
colleague, "that's one of my old patrons."

? + Fiat
*after Denise Riley*

We tumbled in a weird embrace,
wires, ankles, wiper blades.
It was colder inside than out,
and the ? knew the workings,
the vehicle the tenor, the knock
from under and to the left or
coming up from somewhere else,
a condition. This was what
its rumbling meant, ? said, unlinked
to the moss around the inside frame,
damned fiat, its roof window,
all hippy fur and mud,
all goody-2-problems.
It veered and spun and shimmied.
Branches snagged – "it's
like the beginning of Misery",
but ?, with big paws, drew blank,
yawned its padded intensity,
might as well have scratched its eyeball,
"except without the winding
roads and the Champagne."

**Rough**

I have a friend I wish could sleep more soundly. Worked in Subway when I met him but now he's sleeping rough, or if not then just grabbing fast sleep on a friend's sofa or in one of those B&B's for people with nowhere to go to sleep.

He's had a hard time but he's so vague about it I find it difficult to get to the bottom of why - except it's his father and it's his grandmother's fault. They're so good at hating him they could hate him in their sleep. At Subway, he was on a zero hours contract. He didn't get zero hours, of course, but he got so few that they amounted to zero money. He was going for an interview at Kwik Fit, which is what he wants to do. Shortly after we met, he told me he had a lot of fingers in a lot of pies. We were in my car, giving him a lift to Cameron Toll. It was the Wimbledon final. He said he was very hard-working and couldn't sit still. He was living with his grandmother which wasn't perfect but he had somewhere to sleep, not that he needed much sleep. If you're asleep you might as well be dead but whatever. He could rest his head in his grandmother's house when he needed to and because at certain points in certain cycles he was asleep, he wasn't dead. The story as I understand it is that he was maybe given money that he was meant to use to pay the council tax but that he in fact used to get tickets for Reading and Leeds, which lead to him being kicked out of the only place he had to sleep, which if it was a short term arrangement wouldn't cause that many problems because he's a likable guy and makes friends easily (hence we're friends) and I think he made arrangement to sleep on friends' floors for a few weeks or months, rotating them so as not to over irritate. My car at that time had an awful damp smell that I was embarrassed about. There's something wrong with the seals on the doors and so when it rains it leaks and you get little forests of snowy mushroomy mould on the carpets. You hear of these people who sleep every night in their cars. I've slept in my car once or twice and once recently I was in my car getting two or three hours sleep when there was a few raps on the window which woke me obviously from my asleep state and it was a policeman and I was like "oh hello". No, I wish I had been like that but I wasn't and anyway he said, "have you been asleep?" and I groggily nodded and said something affirmatively, virtually still sleeping and he said, "why?" And I said, "oh, I had some trouble at home and wanted some air and I needed some sleep," and he took my number plate and began to radio it in when his superior came over and she said "it's ok – everybody sleeps. No need to radio it in but your lights were on. Have you been drinking?" "Yes," I said, I had been drinking but I hadn't been driving, I had just returned to my car which was parked here from earlier as I had been meeting up with some friends. "OK," she said, "we're going to leave it at that but we could do you for having the ignition on so please don't let me drive back round here and find you sleeping in half an hour." "I won't", I said, "I don't think I could get back to sleep even if I wanted to. I'll walk home. Maybe get the bus. But I doubt I'll sleep. Thank-you, seriously, I appreciate it." A few weeks ago, the last time I met up with him after he said he'd had to have a couple of outdoor sleeps, he had just got a place in a B&B and needed to buy new bedding because the stuff there was all pock marked with cigarette burns and smelled awful. We met at Sainsbury's which he called Tesco when giving me the instructions on where to meet. Near Haymarket. I said he must have done it to put me off the scent but he didn't really get what I meant and just said that he hadn't even realised it wasn't Tesco, even as he stood outside it, half asleep, these hessian bags under his eyes that I really hope don't turn out to be bags for life. I tried to ask him seriously whether he'd made any improvements in the relationship with his family but things, he said, were worse, if anything. He couldn't even get in touch with his mother now. It felt to him like everyone had abandoned him as if they all just woke up from an eighteen year sleep and it was back like he didn't exist any more. I must have been half asleep myself because I asked him about Subway, as if it would be vaguely possible to keep up even a zero hours contract while sleeping rough, sleep the last of his worries, to be honest, washing and cleaning clothes and eating and maintaining a sort of regular appearance more important at the minute. He seemed like he was trying not to sink into accidentally becoming something that he didn't feel he was. It was heart breaking and difficult to see him. I need to get in touch with him.

**Coup de Pied**

These geologists
(umbrella term)
one says *is this on me?*
and the other *no we'll
split it* and me *are you
discussing rocks?*

I don't feel too clever

strewing petals,
seeing individual leaves
a hundred yards away

oozy sumptuous feeling of
thinking it's about to rain
the pounding of expectation

atrial fibrillation, atrial flutter

so mysterious
so mysterious
yesterday's news

and here was me thinking
"foot flirt!"

**Behind a Mustang**

on the friendliest motorway in Britain
the M8
you say "that's a Mustang"
and I say "alright Matt LeBlanc"

I concentrate on driving

we're on our way to an appointment
and you're also texting our friend

"half an hour to go" you say
"oh we'll make it then"
"I meant of the transfusion"

**Two non-starters**

I wanted to write
something like the Mağma al-balāgha
by al-Rāghib al-Isfahānī,
a poetic text of found
phrases and expressions
that sound excessive
but exquisite.
Words like Lucozade,
like Liverance.
I have a thing for "l's".

I wanted to write
something like Harmony Hammond's
*Ledger Drawing Series*, just
loaded words like "Diva"
repeatedly handwritten
on beautiful Twinrocker paper,
school detention-style, written
out till expunged.

## Jaw Drp

On the spectrum of sleaze
I wanted my poetry to be maybe tenth or twelfth
weirdest
the most grommeted
the most bubble-lettering-fonted, perforce perverse
we invented a kind of crowd funder
monetizing and ablaze
between two trees there was a swing
we always suspected the word "lab"
when not used for canine or chemistry
every morning we had to call someone out
before we got called out ourselves
it showed we were with-it
to have spotted something wrong with someone
was the most valuable cultural talent or attribute
newspapers and magazines asked for short stories
but newspapers and magazines by this time meh
I started writing a thesis on the costumes of
Bumble Dawson and intended to use a photo
by Barbara Ker-Symer on the title page.

**Plateau's Laws**

In the ad-break
the denouement
easy to feel crushed
and not like a milkshake

says: no. I'm thinking: I don't know.
a nice bloke but he hovers.
do you ever think to yourself
it's so weird
that you think to yourself:
point
or move your ear
or move your whole head
and then you do

there're lovelinesses
e.g. airy, mathematical charm
Josh Whitehouse's Burberry Advert
film between/across the surface
'partially free boundary'
*Make me do nothing*, by Victoria Redel

been in a kind of bubble
my own little world

dog basket made of foam

sitting on my own knee for comfort
fetching my own sticks

challenge this Llama not to walk towards me
stroke its coat

when you don't watch tv you forget
you lose your authority on what matters

And now you're all thinking
*Who said anything about enjoyment?*

The contours of this space
focusing on the contours of the space
disorienting
I don't know if it still exists -
the queer leaning restaurant
Dalloway in New York
I don't know if queer-leaning is brushing up against the walls
or sitting on the visitor chair
or taking pictures
I bought a scarf (for Jane for her birthday)
Queer is after all a spatial term
*every lifeworld*
*buzzes teems fleets and flirts* slanted
all your furniture
*You are all treating me like furniture*
*I've always thought that needed context* - Sara Ahmed
you treat me like a lampshade with holes in it
the levitating woman by the pond is a reorientation
the fact I can't take photographs is a reorientation
the map of the garden is a reorientation
the old discarded sign in the woods
the yellow hose
*the queer world is a space of entrances,*
*exits, unsystematised lines of acquaintance*

*projecting horizons, typifying examples,*
 *alternate routes, blockages,*
*incommensurate geographies* – Lauren Berlant
the airport this morning
had laminated signs all over it:
"Security is our priority"
the decorations in Charleston
serve a similar purpose:
Queerness is our priority
Queernesses are our priorities
I've always thought design did kind of mean to de-sign
like people devein shrimp
but maybe a laminated sign would do the job just as well
on my tour someone in the group said
"it seems like Clive Bell really became the man of the house"
please please, it seemed like
the staircase creaked
the floor creaked
a laminated sign is wipe clean at least
for today's writing exercise you are a badly
damaged painting and you are writing the
instructions for restoration
someone else inspected the wiring and
wasn't impressed, in their professional perspective
for today's exercise you are a museum writing its
funding application

for a re-enactment called:

## The Pond Aflame

One idea I had for these
poems was I divide the room up into different rooms
little groups
a collective: awwwwwwwww
a flurry of embarrassment
I love embarrassment
It's the untransportability of embarrassment
that keeps this pond aflame
So all of you in your groups I'd
keep constantly asking you to change your function
be a studio / be a bedroom / be a study
get into character
be a firework display
now be a kiln
now be a crib
now be a swimming pool, from pond overflow
now be a Pither stove
You'd have loved this I swear
it'd be so much fun
I'm almost changing my mind about not doing it
Maybe it's a little late
in "Queer Phenomenology: Objects, Orientations,
    Others",
Ahmed writes that she's interested in bringing what's
*behind* to the *front*... her example is the writing
table

what is *background* here?
now be a colander lamp shade
now be a pottery head
now all please be a pond
and the fish in the water
Angelica – *on the wall it looked like cooked lobster but
    it later paled to salmon*
So please be a pond this minute
your mouths opening and closing
breathless in wonder

## *Male Nude*, 1934, Duncan Grant

Reuben notices the damage to the paint
He has a keen eye
I notice the pecs
The pattern of the painty flesh
My plan for redecoration includes an ombre staircase
And silver glitter all over that table with the sweat ring
This is not to say that you have to leave home for things
To be disoriented or reoriented, *homes too can be giddy places*,
*where things are not always held in place, and homes can move, as we do.*
Before we go in a big song and dance is made about how
The artists (air quotes) never owned this house,
Always rented always leased
I love air quotes
A kind of yoga in miniature
Song and dance was figurative there but
I just watched the Anne Hathaway, Russell Crowe,
Hugh Jackman, etc *Les Miserables* so for today's writing
exercise I want you all to write a review
Of the "song and dance" about how they never owned
the house.
You have until the end.
Answers on a postcard
The nudes in the last room
The studio

Orientations are about the intimacy of bodies and their places
The paint that seems to create the body is also where the atmosphere
Creates an impression
Just think of goosebumps
Think of shape and pattern
Radiator Cover, circa 1928, wool, glass beads, linen upper frieze, velcro, designed by Humphrey Slater, made by Vanessa Bell
I went to the Highland Show
And there was a bird of prey display
Including an eagle
And the falconer described one time
When the eagle grabbed him by the head in its tallons
And shook him like a 14 stone fish

**Streusel Topping**

Sometimes I think of a poet's new collection
as a Spring / Summer launch - moody and cool
sometimes it seems like a
foam / book party is
a good idea
I really enjoyed *Love, Simon* and cried
like the biggest lettuce ever grown
in Scotland but still:
why do they live in such big houses?
I'm going to write something called *A
Few Yes Please Do Why The Fuck Nots*
frenemy vibe boiling over
a poem is a birthday cake
a wavy birthday cake in
pastel but with your face
and when you cut it
your skin peels off
all sugar all daddy
the style of reading
where you lick your finger
to turn the page
and it's your birthday
after every bite

**Area Scatter**
*for Area Scatter of the Ugwu Anya Egbulam Musical Group*

eye about to do damage
                decides not to
                because charm, muscle, sweets
you think stuff can't get worse but
   new fucking horrible things are in pre-production all
    the time
                this song about being a small man
                unhappy until you meet someone smaller
you roll on the floor and only then they start to laugh
                smile because they just remembered
                what smile because they're kings and queens
   Area Scatter never stopped being a civil servant
   just found new ways to tinkle a thumb new
   ways
   let's do it again
   I dream Area Scatter is
   like a hammer on the block
   still a love
   still scattering area
   Area Scatter we love you, reappear before us
And tell us where you've been
Make us love you by being more rad than we thought
   possible

**This is my hot take**

Yayoi Kusama's 1968 *Homosexual Wedding*
complete with dot-orgy two-person costume
for bride and groom at the Church of Self
Obliteration, and at which all guests were
expected to participate, and where presiding
Kusama ensured consummation, this piece
isn't about gay marriage.

Dorothea Tanning's 1948 *On Time and Off Time* ,
which is a painting with a strange wooden looking
construction, a smoking fire with an eye in it,
a sunflower, two animal forms and a woman blindfolded
blowing bubbles against a blue background,
isn't about time …

Mira Schor's 'Double Bubble' (1992), an
Oil on linen with a lilac ground, a beautiful
Ethereal bubble tapering at the right hand
side and filling the whole canvas at its widest
contains the head of a penis, with a little
bead like bubble from its meatus, this piece
is definitely about bubbles…

# oOo Bubbling Over oOo

**Dream Fettucine**
with Maria Sledmere

dear colin,

very sorry to bother you but I wanted to send you something I've been working on in advance of our next supervision, getting anxious about the APR, everyone talking about the APR and only recently I discovered they weren't referring to mortgages — I thought everyone on the PhD was so grown-up and worried about MORTGAGES when actually they just wanted to progress or something.

this is sorta relevant because my poem is about fettuccine, which feels like the sort of thing people with mortgages eat. or maybe academics, after strenuous conferences. I know you're already thinking why is Maria writing about fettuccine, like what's that got to do with the a n t h r o p o c e n e. maybe because my name is sort of italian. honestly though, I can't say much more about it beyond the fact that it appeared in my dream, I dreamt you were looking for poems about fettuccine and rolled over and in the mirror in the next dream I was fourteen and blonde again and my hair was like a tangle of pasta, and if I lifted one strand the rest fell into endless loops. which is sort of how I feel when I think about my PhD! maybe I shouldn't be discouraged by this dream.

(I'll admit I did just google anthropocene fettuccine and I found a meme called Trump Instant Noodles which wasn't what I was looking for at all).

ANYWAY, here is my poem, I'm so sorry:

**Little Ribbons**

Here two strands of pasta diverge
and sorry for each of us
somebody on twitter said your sleep is delicious

and long I spun bundles of light
with creamy lexicons of hair and higher carbs

dreaming these emails of curly Italian slogans
seasoned with nutmeg, salt
and artisanal naps

I was reading about hookworms
and luxury solutions, ash trees,
calorie count software
and stylish microbials

Imagine that ribbon just rising inside you

suppose it all dies back, they twirl us
clean on the end of a fork

We didn't choose them
the people with our bodies
adorning their cutlery

(my brother went gluten-free for winter)

I relate to you, eons later
the annual percentage rate of a poem
and one fat egg in credit

The recipe says: what makes the difference
is the way you add the parmesan—
less is always more.

{{emoji spaghetti}}

please can you let me know what you think of the poem, I'm bracing
myself, I wondered if you noticed any ecological flavours or is this
just pure consumer anxiety and by the way, the secret is I'm still
trying to be vegan & failing at the point of cheese and chocolate.
Does any of this connect to our discussion of queer intimacies,
I'm not sure. Do you know anyone with a pasta machine? Maybe I
should ask the other supervisors.

all kindest wishes,maria


Buonjourno Alfredo!

And sorry for the delay. Almost said decay there. On the hour every
hour is a beautiful idea (was it mine? It's mixing with all the carbs).
It's not sustainable for me but when did that stop anything. I said
those letters earlier right? APR. I feel like don't be anxious about it.
Isnt don't be anxious the worst bit of advice when anxious? Bring us

a plate of Fettuccine and we'll be paper in your hands. You could rip us up. I'm saying we like I have influence but seriously if anything went awry in your APR I'd get up and leave this so-called restaurant because I wouldn't care to ingest anything on the menu any longer. I'm now confused whether I dreamed about your Fettuccine or you dreamed about how I wanted to read Fettuccine poems. Your ribbons. Can you send me over some props like a big pepper grinder and a tablecloth and a bottle of wine? Or one with a candle in it? Your poem is gorgeous. Here's my one sentence critique: it should have been in Angel Hair, the Poetry magazine. The ecological flavours are more than a garnish. Though I barely touch them myself, as you know. For me the line about the curly slogans is the dish on which the whole thing slips off. The Med is a sentence. A comma as curl. As far as imagining the ribbon - yes I'm with you I think but I don't use 00 grade flour. I prefer a mealier texture. I should give up Gluten. I've got this new personal trainer who is helluva persistent. Don't tell the Scottish Graduate School but there's a module I'm not sure I got to in Supervisor Training so please tell me if this seems way off base but I wondered if you'd take a look at a poem I've been working on? It's called:

## You know Justin Bieber kept a Cappucin Monkey - what if it was actually a Fettuccin Monkey?

Stretching across
to somebody who's
swimming
or can you protect me

with some kind of

    speedo canopy

as per

When Elvis got

a cough cough

I got a cough cough

I mean can you protect me

too

weird diseases

bread and butter

protection sucks

an email

makes me look like

a bad poet and bad teacher of poetry

I'm a swishing size of a

person a person size of a

swish and you make me

Or if I could just face up to certain aspects

of my life that cause me a lot of trouble


Less isn't always more!

Wishes,

Colin


Also - I have a pasta machine! But I'm spread a little thin to use it. A rolling pin can apparently suffice, in a pinch.

Ciao Colin! I wanted to say a proper good morning but I was worried about messing up the pronunciation. I just dreamt I was serving you plateful after plateful of tumbling carbs at a restaurant, the walls were Yves Klein blue and they were playing Nine Inch Nails really loudly, like in a movie. Oh and you were sitting with Bernadette Mayer, at least I think it was her, you could tell from the braids, and sharing a bottle of wine that just said SUPER TUSCAN on the label. I have been reading a lot of what she says about hunger. I am so grateful for your solidarity vis a vis possible APR table drama and will channel that confidence when I find myself in front of a panel, tangled; but also I will bring a Rennie's for you just in case. Maybe I need to hone my skills in the kitchen: embrace this chiasmus between cooking and good prose. It's all about patience. I used to work with a lovely Italian boy called Claudio and one day we were at the park and he came over and offered us barbecued pasta, and proceeded to read verse from his epic play about the triumph of love right there on the hill, and I thought there was clearly some imperative relationship between the poetry and the pasta, like that sort of desire was only sustainable with carbs, and charred carbs especially.

Anyway thank you for your thoughts on the poem, and Angel Hair would be gorgeous: I am reimagining angelheaded hipsters as waiters and waitresses with haloes of ribbony fettuccine. I think sometimes I overdo the ecopoetic garnish, like adding too much garden or garlic. I was reading your 'Butterflies and Funding Bodies' in A Plume last night: 'Barely anyone wrote anything that wasn't ecopoetics' and dreams full of 'wolf howls and bird song', which also made me think of Ginsberg's 'Howl' and oddly, Bergson, and therefore snowballs. Durational memory rolling and rolling like someone laying a carpet of grass down in reverse. Mealier textures, yes. You know you can buy 'Ancient Grain' rice cakes in Morrisons; I think they're made out of ground-up pyramids and ruins, or maybe just chia seeds. They're probably gluten-free. What would a gluten-free or low-cal poem look like? I've been wondering for ages. I keep binging on midnight lines and hurting my stomach, or maybe that's just the Lisa Robertson, she's so damn sumptuous. Her poems are like sun-ripened tomatoes set to slow cook, a sweet and nourishing sauce that makes you want more and more.

You know Justin Bieber once got a misdemeanour charge for throwing eggs at his neighbour's house. I guess he was monkeying around and/or trying to make architectural fettuccine, but he was clearly going the wrong way about it and besides you also need flour.

Don't tell anyone but I also missed the workshop on 'Developing a Relationship with Your Supervisor' so who knows about etiquette. Your poem is so beautiful I feel like it's unravelling, satisfying like those 'How to' homemade pasta webpages, with images and everything, and its texture is slippy and bitty at once, there's a good grain to it. It's also super liquid and shimmery even, like Arthur Russell's 'Let's Go Swimming', which is like wearing a turquoise bathing suit and knowing all the rhythms of other people's muscles. I think a lot about tenderness in poetry and how we can exercise tenderness in lines. I like how the swish might be a Nike logo wrestling with the Lacoste crocodile from Click + Collect.

Um here is a little sappy midweek poem:

**Lo-fi ideals**

*The Guardian* referred to a grab-back collection
of Belle & Sebastian movies as
a little over-cute at times
I think about that a lot
like apparently they just cook pasta
and play with cuddly toys in the bath
Is that being candid
like when you order the endearing wrong thing
on the menu
or come back from the supermarket
without milk, but
you have a really long list of nice things
to give as receipt
Sometimes I worry that candy
gives you candida, but

I'm not sure what that means
Sometimes I miss all my friends
I want to mix them into sugary super-8s
who needs milk anyway
we should just do something pretty.


With warmth,

Maria


p.s. When I hand in my final thesis I expect you to put it through the pasta machine and THEN we can send it to Angel Hair, maybe.

Oh and I don't have a tablecloth sadly but maybe I could wear gingham and you could wear a raspberry sweater in honour of Angel Hair O'Hara?


Dear Nigel Slater, I read with interest your cookery column in the Guardian. Have you read my poem "Colin" from Too Ok, where I swap out "Maria" for my own name - and I actually switch in boy for girl although that was back in 2009 or something and ten years later I might be less pedantic. I felt like I'd tried a lot of pasta - but your talk of Claudio and his Barbecued Pasta has alerted me to a blind spot - like when it suddenly twigs - hey wait a second - why weren't they in the New American Poetry? (Actually typed Piety there) and why weren't they? Bring the Rennie's for Steve - I can already see this is going to get overly stretchy. I bought pasta from Marks and Spencer's last night - it was a kind of tagliatelle with truffle - the truffle actually in the pasta, which was dried and came in a big box. I don't actually go nuts for truffle but it looked like the pasta strands were going to be enormous. When I opened them, there was cardboard fitted so there was a gap and they weren't nearly as thread-like as they seemed. I could barely bring myself to cook them but cook them I did. I've been reading Emily Petit's Poem "How to be irresponsible": "I'm obsessed with an old problem and I have a brand new megaphone". "I let the lions out too, but I'm not the zookeeper". Oh Butterflies and Funding Bodies. I wasn't archaeologically digging. I was meaning (having learnt as much from you) that thinking ecologically can be thinking in forms other than a wolf howl. Somebody wrote to me yesterday, I'm not going to say who because I invited them to the thing on Saturday. Maybe you know them. They told me they didn't like my poems two years ago but now they do. They said they had a new appreciation for trash. They want to do a PhD - not in flattery I don't think. In creative writing. A PhD in Flattery. From the Centre for Pleasure. I just figured out what APR stands for. I wonder if Bieber is more of a chef than you give him credit for? "All his body was tender / But most of it did not know" - Kathleen Fraser. You'd have to reform Angel Hair in order to get permission to send your poem there. Write to Anne Waldman and see what she says. Your poem isn't sappier than it needs to be - it needs to be sappy right at the end. Any poem that has ideals in the title needs to be sappy right at the end. (it's lucky I'm here to sprinkle all this advice-Parmesan). Is it I also need someone to taste the wine before pouring when the buds are misaligned. There is an imperative relationship between poetry and pasta because etymologically pasta means paste and fettuccine has something to do with slice. So, I'm sending you this antipasti:

5 Star Review

Does anyone want me to eat right now?
Eat something from my bag or my pocket.
Or from the floor? Or from your bags? I
could select someone and start hunting
through their bag for food. I like
fettuccine. Or your pockets? A mint or a
smartie or pastille of some kind? Or
pretend I'm eating? Or beg you for food?

Maybe some of you could start throwing food
my direction and I actually won't want it
because I'm on a diet. But I'd eat some to
be polite.

{[emoji knife + fork | salt | glass of milk | baby's bottle | mixing bowl | serving spoon | glass of wine}}


Thrown,

Colin

P.S What's your idea of a good sauce? Do you slice more or paste more? Is an APR a necessary evil, a necessary good, an unnecessary evil or an unnecessary good? Can you make yourself more or less tender and if you did either of those would your poems be more or less tender? Candida the Musical would you go or avoid?

Dear Colin,

It's with great pleasure that I open your letter from the comfort of my kitchen garden. I have always wanted to receive a letter from an eminent poet especially one who shares deep-rooted feelings for mycelial cuisine. I have this recipe for a howling arrabiata you might like. A penne for your pen!

Best regards,

Nigel

{{emoji spaghetti}}

Hi Colin,

I am so glad you switched Maria for Colin back in 2009 because there are already far too many Maria songs on the market, I was a much serenaded waitress. Middle-aged men often believe their Sancerre will come quicker with a certain tremolo. And then, click, click! I'm so sorry Steve we are finishing shortly. I wish I'd seen your beautiful tagliatelle; M&S dinners are so iconic, have you ever eaten one in the bath? Imagine you could scoop all the handwriting out of a book and drape it on a dish. That would be a PhD in pleasure. I wouldn't eat Woolf's writing — far too loopy — but maybe I'd go for jagged Kafka or slender Emily's. Buzzfeed describes it as 'language from another planet'! Now that's a dish to knock off your anthropos! Bieber's Tendy Body is the name of my slowcore punk band that nobody knows about. One of many culinary aporia you actually don't need to try is the deconstructed lemon meringue from our 2015 Christmas menu. You can't make Derrida jokes on average drunkards. I was reading this bit from Rodefer's Four Lectures where he's talking about art and how what we really want is the frame: 'He puts titles on to prove he has a mind. The school of spaghetti'. I regret putting titles on all my poems, like little kitsch place cards. Ann Charter once said Jack Kerouac didn't remember her at 'Ginsberg's party eating spaghetti'; well he would if she'd had a place card, maybe. I don't know, sounds too bourgie. Would we remember ourselves better as dishes instead?

**Pre-theatre**

Honestly you should try the new
Colin we have on our menu
So highly commended
This Colin is excellent with camembert
or you could sample the Colin croutes!
I've heard folks describe a tender Aries
that comes with a kick. Yes, notes

of cracked black pepper and cedar
You know the good burnt sugar
to finish a creme brulee?
I really recommend the second Colin
after you've tried the first
One can't just try a single Colin!
We have a special offer on Colins
with your name written all over it
Just give me a shout if you want more Colin
I'll be over there, grating parmesan quietly.

{{emoji cheese with holes in}}

In answer to your last question, I would only see Candida the opera because I like the idea of microbes screaming at me in asynchrony. Is the body a unity of time and place and if not does it fail as drama?

Confused,
Maria


p.s.

Have you ever noticed a piece of fettuccine is also a mobius strip? I mean we could go on and on with this.

**Today**

(Ok this is me now as in the Rea me... what are we going to do on stage? Read the whole thing? Is it too long? Is it done? Do we need to have it on one long piece of paper and put it through the pasta machine? I dunno what this but I like it a lot... should we edit? Is this bit going to be read aloud?I feel like I need to send this to the other supervisors to get their feedback?!) I have a weird desire to print something out and have it available as a takeaway for everyone???

Like menu a la carts 15:51

rte* 15:51

## WOOLF BUBBLES FOR COLIN HERD ON HIS BIRTHDAY 28 MARCH 2019 by Jane Goldman

fizzled like effervescing water
                , leaving a little border of bubbles
                and foam on either side.
                    round and round; the bubbles which
                        swam and clustered
                    saw again the bubbles meeting
                something about bubbles
            You can't see my bubble; I can't see yours;
                "A nice streaky bubble yours must be!"
        "And supposing my bubble could run into
someone else's bubble—"
"And they both burst?"
                    She rose light as a bubble to her seat.
        cistern overflowing; water bubbling
            up would bubble an irresponsible optimism.
                each word falling like a disc new cut,
            not a hubble-bubble of small smooth coins s
    as the boy stood still came
                        bubbling from his pipe,
            a frail quivering sound,
a voice bubbling up without direction,
            l breeze the ancient song bubbled up
                still the old bubbling burbling song,
            , like a kettle on the hob; bubbling,
murmuring, always busy,

>            her sentence bubbled away drip, drip, drip,
>                 like a contented tap left running.
>            out of that pernicious hubble-bubble if it
> were only
>            to now a weed, now a straw, now a bubble,
>            she felt again, sinking deeper, 00000000
>        away in green cascades, in bubbles, in cataracts.
>            the bubbles would be seen to be firmly fixed;
>       the red, thick stream of life again; bubbling, dripping;
>             and we rise, and our eyes (for how handy
> a rhyme
>      is to pass us safe over the awkward transition from
> death to life) fall on
>        "Bubbles form on the floor of the saucepan," said
> Jinny.
>         "Then they rise, quicker and quicker, in a silver
> chain to the top."
>         I will drop a stone in and see bubbles rise from
> the depths of the sea.
>     Up they bubble—images.
>         One floats, too, as if one were that bubble;
>      one is freed; I have escaped, one feels.
> Even the chubby little boys (Dalton, Larpent and Baker)
>     feel the same abandonment. They like this better
> than the cricket.
>     They catch the phrases as they bubble.
> The bubbles are rising like the silver bubbles from the
> floor

of a saucepan; image on top of image.

    Bernard, in public, bubbles; in private, is secretive.
       More and more bubbles
into my mind as I talk, images and images.

    That is, I am a natural coiner of words,

      a blower of bubbles through one thing and another.

    Toys I twist, bubbles I blow, one ring passing through
        another.

  Bubbling and chuckling they carried little bits of straw

    and twig to the dark knots in the higher branches
of the trees.

    And as I move, surrounded, included and taking
part,

      the usual phrases begin to bubble up, and I wish to
free

      these bubbles from the trap-door in my head,

      and direct my steps therefore towards that man,

        the back of whose head is half familiar to me.

           The little boys used to feel

  "That's a good one, that's a good one", as the
phrases

    bubbled up from my lips under the elm trees

    in the playing-fields. They too bubbled up; they
also escaped
with my phrases.

    Yet there are moments when the walls of the mind
grow thin;

    when nothing is unabsorbed, and I could fancy

that we might blow so vast a bubble that the sun might set
and rise in it and we might take the blue of midday
and the black of midnight and be cast off and escape
   from here and now.
faces that bubble up out of the doors of the Tube, and many
Whatever sentence I extract whole and entire from this cauldron
is only a string of six little fish that let themselves be caught
while a million others leap and sizzle, making the cauldron
   bubble like boiling silver, and slip through my fingers.

   Faces recur, faces and faces—they press their beauty to the walls of my bubble—Neville, Susan, Louis, Jinny, Rhoda and a thousand others.

   It bubbled with grey spots that went in and out.
the face was still there, bubbling in and out,
     There were no bubbles on the water yet.
       The little bubbles kept rising to the top and
      exploding. He watched them rise and explode.
He watched the bubbles rising in the yellow liquid. For them
   For him a life modelled on the jet (he was watching
   the bubbles rise), on the spring, of the hard leaping
fountain; another life; a different life. Not halls and

but at the same time spread out, make a new ripple
   in human consciousness, be the bubble and the stream, the stream and the bubble—myself and the world together—

                                      he raised his glass.
   He surveyed the thin yellow liquid in which the bubbles rose more slowly, one by one.
        He saw again the glass with the bubbles rising;
   The bubbles had ceased to rise. The wine was clear and still.
   Then they went in to lunch, and Mrs. Manresa bubbled up,
A spring of feeling bubbled up through her mud.

Syllabubble

oOo

This is a book for Jeffrey Robinson's writings on The Fancy, for the bubbles in Anna Laetita Barbauld's poem 'Washing Day', where verse is bubbles and we know it. This is a book for Boris Vian, *Foam of the Daze*, the moments when the character Colin makes clusters of soapy bubbles.

oOo

This book is for Kamau Brathwaite, *Sun Poem*, and Denise Levertov 'Song for Ishtar', and for Denise Levertov's 'Prologue: An Interim', and for King Princess's music video for 'Holy', and for Verner Panton's Wall Bubbles and for Chrystos 'Soap Bubbles' and for Jack Smith saying "I'm the Bubble Goddess" then "Tell me the truth has the camera started".

oOo             oOo

This is a book for Francis Ponge's "ballet of veils, of floating sashes, whirling, eddying, falling back, self-enfolding, self-unfolding" in *Soap*, for Abu Nuwas's many descriptions of the bubbles of wine – for wishing to be the bubbles in the wine your crush is about to ingest.

oOo   oOo

This is a book for Eileen Myles's writing on queer foam in *Afterglow (A Dog Memoir)* and for C. V. Boys, *Soap Bubbles and the Forces that Mould them*, which Elizabeth Bishop loved and carried around.

oOo

oOo

This is a book for Zhu Ming, bubble performances from 1994 to the present, including: *11$^{th}$ May 1994; 14$^{th}$ May 1994; 27$^{th}$ December 1994; Liquid Sea Performance 2003*

oOo

This is a book for  Keats who's very very bubbly when he wants to be. This is a book for Kim Seung-Hee, whose work is very bubbly too. And CA Conrad's 'Power Sissy Intervention'

oOo

oOo            oOo

For John Ashbery's poem 'The Skaters' and for Jenny Holzer, *Soap Bubble,* Diagrams, for Edwin Arlington Robinson's 'Dear Friends', Rembrandt Harmensz van Rijn, *Cupid with the Soap Bubble*, (1634), Pieter Bruegel the Elder, *Children's Games*, (1560), Frank O'Hara's 'Ducal Days', for Anne Waldman's The Structure of the World Compared to a Soapbubble, for Amy Lowell's 'Peach-color to a Soap-bubble', for Joseph Plateau on soap bubbles, for Idea Vilariño whose bubbles burst in the end.

oOo

            oOo            oOo

oOo

For the character Professor Horne from Ursula LeGuin, *Searoad: Chronicles of Klatsand* in which "each foam billow, each foam pillow shivers under the wind shakes quivers, inescapably feminine though not at all female.... Feeble, fatuous, flabby, helpless mammocks of porous lard, all that men despise and paint and write about in women, ... Each blob, peak, flake of foam is an entity, a brief being "

oOo

"All men are bubbles"

William Whitehead, 'Creusa, Queen of Athens', (1754)

oOo

                                      oOo oOo oOo

oOo

This book is for Ai Weiwei, *Bubble*, and Peter Sloterdijk, *Bubbles*, for Umberto Saba's *Light and Airy Things*, for Thomas Couture's 'Soap Bubbles' and for Jean Siméon Chardin's 'Soap Bubbles'

oOo

"Look at the soapy bubbles of my tears, on every side"
    Hāfez (1325 - 1390), translated by Julie Meisami

oOo

Edward Steichen, 'The Brass Bowl', (1906)
Edward Steichen, 'Still Life with Sink and Soap', (1930)
Edward Steichen, 'Woodbury Soap', (1935)

oOo

Roy Mack (dir), *Bubbles* (1930), first screen appearance of Judy Garland

oOo

"sinking bewildered of hand, of foot, of lip
   nude, thinking
laughter burnished brighter than hate

                                      Goodbye.
                   André Breton said that
                             what a shit!
Now he's gone!
                   up bubbles all his amorous breath
                   & Monograph on Infidelity entitled
                         The Living Dream"
- Ted Berrigan from *Bean Spasms* (1967)

oOo

oOo      oOo                    oOo oOo oOo

Ed Ruscha, 'Another Hollywood Dream Bubble Popped', (1976)

oOo

oOo

"Blowing bubbles out of a pipe gives the feeling of the rapid crowd of ideas and scenes which blew out of mind, so that my lips seemed syllabling of their own accord as I walked. What blew the bubbles. Why then? I have no notion"
    Virginia Woolf on the composition of
    *To the Lighthouse* in 'A Sketch of the Past', 1939

oOo

John Everett Millais, *Bubbles*, (1886)

oOo                oOo

oOo

oOo
oOo     oOo

Mira Schor, *Double Bubble*, (1992)

oOo


"Lumps, bumps, bulbs, bubbles, bulges, slits, turds,

coils, craters, wrinkles, and holes"

Elaine Showalter on Louise Bourgeois, Tate Etc, (2007)

Printed in Great Britain
by Amazon